Upward Spiral
Poems of Opening and Renewal

Upward Spiral
Poems of Opening and Renewal

Shelly Barnett
Leonore Hildebrandt
Pamela Warren Williams
Lynne Zotalis

Upward Spiral Collective
Silver City, New Mexico

Upward Spiral
Poems of Opening and Renewal

ISBN 9798860313897
Publisher: Upward Spiral Collective
Silver City, New Mexico
Printed in the United States of America
First Edition
Copyright ©2023
Shelly Barnett
Leonore Hildebrandt
Pamela Warren Williams
Lynne Zotalis

Leonore Hildebrandt's poem, Centers of Balance was previously published in Plant Human Quarterly.

Lynne Zotalis 's Earth Bereft and Finding Earth's Treasure were previously published in Poetic Bond IX. Loquacious Limbs was previously published in Nature 20/20

Come out here where the roses have opened.
Let soul and world meet.
—Rumi

Table of Contents

Earth

Fire

Air

Water

Earth

Centers of Balance

She tries to feel what's beautiful
with a quiet mind—but thought
opens her to the earth's honed
geometry. See how the sunflower's
outer petals, maroon and orange,
frame the flowerhead, and its center
the disc florets, packed close—
golden ratio, the Fibonacci sequence—
their angles perfect for growing
the greatest sum of seeds.
In every spiral's numerical center,
a promise. And she, too, watching—
the double helix, a loaded spring,
her futures coiled and ready.

—Leonore Hildebrandt

Posterity Planning

I'm planting, I tell my sister. She points to the obvious—
not my first attempt. But I know more now.
About this difficult land.
The propensity for withering or being consumed
by some new breed of intruders. Feeling a
homesteader, with the legacy of determination and grit,
I muster their resolve.
Planting for posterity, I consider what progress
I may witness, promising to research projected growth.
What was that fir tree that sprang up over the wall
in only my three-year residency in investment suburbia?
Hopefully, some consolation for the loss of
all those blighted fruit trees...
As I smile now at the Flame Sumac
in its first autumn glow, I continue to
face forward whenever possible.

—Pamela Warren Williams

Strength of a Daffodil

The end of wintering,
offers random days of almost Spring.
Earth is taunted by hours of spontaneous sun,
temperatures rising above the degrees
that bring a few days of freeze.

Another snow day imminent,
the early budding blooms of the determined daffodils
bring worry, then hope,
gathering their leaves inward
and bow their flowering heads
in collective sheltering.

Blanketed in fresh snow,
the tiny mounds become survival mysteries of Nature.
Roots send up warmth from their spindly toes
that burrow deeply in the cloak
of Mother Earth.

The afternoon thaws
quench the thirst of the resilient stems,
as newly birthed vibrant yellow petal cups
join the laughing survivors
 in sun-worshipping solidarity.

Adamant daffodils
offering roots of comfort, leaves of shelter,
and blossoms of hope,
as they bloom in times of uncertainty,
showing their persistence to the world.

—Shelly Barnett

Finding Earth's Treasure

our mother's labor

effortless, taken for granted

as seasons evolve

wind shuddered boughs stretch from rolling hills

atop white mantle— cornfield's languid sleep

the repose of energy spent producing bounteous yield

driftless Mississippi River bluffs

birth new life in eagle's eyrie

where milkweed fairies flit free to propagate

nourishing millions of monarchs

fueling their 3,000 mile flight from

high mountain Michoacán forests

to Canada in a passage

by four generations

in two miraculous months—

some say our planet's survival depends on theirs

our existence reliant on them

as much as   air   water   earth

—Lynne Zotalis

Earth Bereft

fall descends

tenacious leaves cling

to naked limbs   shivering

September's   final   dance

while

desolate arms   bid adieu

to autumn eve's whispered song

lulling   Mother   earth

to   winter's   sleep

on a frost-laden

carpet

—Lynne Zotalis

Liminal Dusk

Perhaps fleeting musings on the potential
for last times. Even down to this being
the likely last time to polish these beloved boots
with their stitching decaying
and their rubber soles calcifying.
It's all alchemy in one form or another.
Entering the limbo state of resolution.
The letting go of that future, the possibilities,
the planning, the banal and the magnificent both.
The focused labor of remaining in the moment,
no matter its agony.
Whether custodial or sacred in nature,
reading you a poem or plotting your cremation.
The knowing of how precious each shared second.

In the background of this pageant of souls lurks inevitability.
Biding until the ball drops. The other shoe.
Whether through the turmoil of struggle for this life
or placid surrender, we are untrained
for either this transition or the next liminal space.
While glancing over one's shoulder into the abyss,
it remains unfathomable until ascension to this realm.
An initiate to this process, familiar self dissolving,
as if a heavy door slammed firmly shut between us.
The sunshine, the dog, the industrious creative hands all assuaging.

Angels in attendance, always.

—Pamela Warren Williams

Earth is Not Your Garden

Without thinking, you find a rhythm
on the trail that encircles the cone-shaped mountain.
There are muddy stretches. Rocks, drop-offs, roots, thorns.

Inscribed on the sloping land is a loveliness
that does not name itself.

And you are in it—moving—
you look up toward the hills, the sky—
you are reckless, you want it all—to breathe it, embrace it,

become the plants, the land, clouds,
air currents, dust and distance.

Earth travels the vacuum of space. Quietly
it rotates its insects, forests, and far poles—
what to do with this knowledge?

You lie down and rest, loving the earth.
Sun holds still as the trail descends into shadow.

Earth is not your garden, not your mother—it just is.
The rocky ledge beneath your body doesn't care
about your days of trouble, your days of glory.

But you are made to care.
You live in a place where caring is possible.

When you come back to the trailhead, you stand
exactly where you started. Nothing else is the same
in the unconcerned workings of the universe.

You have become part of the mountain's story.
Did you leave traces of joy?

Earth is spinning you into a goodness
only you and I are capable of making up.

—Leonore Hildebrandt

Terra Firma Antiquity

I told him to bring me some dirt.
Dirt? He asked.
Terra firma. Grecian dirt.
Created from dust of the earth,
scripture or hearsay? To dirt we return, dust to dust
I asked him for dirt

Grandpa Aristides Pontelli Zotalis was born
in the village Kremasti in northern Greece.
Jason made the pilgrimage his grandpa never could.
Back to the homeland.   Land.
The profusion of relatives treasuring,
living their heritage   ancestry intact and revered
dating to the 12 century BC.   Their land.
He shared a picture of the door of the house
his grandpa lived in. I asked Jason Aristides Zotalis
to bring me some dirt.   He got it,   the symbolism,
sending me a picture of an uncle Zotalis
scooping dirt into a container.
I don't think I will ever go there   only being married to it,
Jason, Jonathan, Joy and Alexis Zotalis own the blood roots,
marrow from Greek dirt, coursing through arteries.

Humans and earth form an intimate crucial bond   soil
containing massive amounts of DNA.
Scientists can figure out ancient strains from modern ones
in the land so alive with history's rich genetic code.

Humus: The Latin word for earth and soil
is the same root word for human,
soil closely connected to culture and civilization
of particular ethnic groups living in a given place
and recording how the collapse of soil is directly linked
to the breakdown of culture, livelihood and health.

I do not know what I will do with my dirt,   smell it
slide my fingers into it   listen
in time   it will tell me where it needs to be
in time.

—Lynne Zotalis

She Carries Her Mother

She emerges from a single ray
that illuminates a family of trees.
Swirling in the dank forest clearing,
her silver hair shimmers
in and out of sunlight.

Gently spiraling to the ground,
she listens closely as
her hands dig the dirt amidst the decaying leaves—
fingers find the roots
of the bark-stripped towers.

Feeling the pulse of despair,
she wipes the ground with the folds of her skirt,
and gathers muddied fabric
in the cradle of her arms.

She whispers,
"Dearest Mother,
I shall carry forth
your fears and tears
everywhere I go.
I will share your tales of
beginnings and gifts of life
with all who walk across your skin.
I shall tell the old and young
to spread the word of your wants."

"Please rest now from your purging and cleansing.
Let us heal you and hold you,
as we carry you back to where
you can touch the sky once again."

—Shelly Barnett

Fire

Painting the Cave

Close to the entrance, a small fire.
Smoke bites the air. She is drawing animals—

fierce, wondrous. Bison and horse.
Bighorn sheep. Wolf. Looming high,
their limbs free-scale the quivering stone.

She feels herself sized up:
who is she—what kind of creature?

Her fingers muddle with pigments and coal
toward movement, vigor, breath. Unbounded,
a hare runs over the rock's ancient face.

She stands and picks up a charred stick,
finds that it wants to point up, circle

outward—a spiral's sacristy—a window
for the cave's dark ceiling. As always
the lion's ears point toward the future.

—Leonore Hildebrandt

Dragon Breath Orange

Tinderbox Town
no warning
as life is sucked
from its collective lungs.

Flames dance in darkness
seeking direction from ocean breezes
becoming hurricane force.
Mountain sunrise hues
instantly turning dragon breath orange.

Roads become swift tongues of fire
while the ocean waves' foamy fingers
beckon to the only way out.
Community floats for hours
on rafts of disbelief
with rudders of hope,
as ashes of their lives descend
to sting burning skin, crying eyes,
broken hearts and heavy minds.

Now Islanders want hulihia...
a turning, the change to return
to the natural cycle
that has been
deeply disturbed,
ready to build
new expectations
for the future.

Hope for hulihia.

—Shelly Barnett

Having Lost Count of How Many Fires

A wall of flames looming behind those
decorative iron gates is a never imagined intruder.
Footage shows an inconceivable night flight
on a burning road through a gauntlet
of billowing flames. Water. So much water.
And the chemicals offered, too. Sprayed and dropped and
uncontained still. An hour to the west,
my brother speculates,
tearing up. Imagining what
those long curls of ash on his car may once have been.
We are all in deep prayer, fragile and checking in
with each other more often than usual.
Left to consider, what would we choose to save
if the crisis were our own?

The beloved Brown House, full of generations
of memories, is miraculously spared,
a tiny sliver amidst miles and miles of devastation.
I sigh for the dear heirloom Cecile Bruner roses.
Grasping fingers of that fire surrounded
the caretaker's house on three sides. No one is
certain yet if the lush acres of gardens and orchards survived.
Endless mysteries rest in the hands
of battalions of heroes from as far away as Australia.
At least prisoners can now have a future in California.

In the heart of earthquake country,
we were always promising to put the evac bag together.
Water. Meds and sentiment. Records of one's life.
Take the dog, first.

Gratitude for all my facts now safely in the mysterious cloud.
And for the wise counsel that too much sentimentality
steals from the present.
I pause in praise for all that has been mine.
How much can I hold to take with me?

I hold vivid memories still of the Oakland hills fire.
Was that our trial run for all this carnage?
Only time to grab the pets and
a random stack of paintings by the front door.

Later images showed the priceless Macchiarini
bronze sculpture melted into the hot earth.
Writers lost entire manuscripts.
We all hold each other so dear now.

—Pamela Warren Williams

Fireflies, Lightning Bugs, Glowworms, Oh My!

"Nana," they asked me, "do you believe in fairies?"

"Yes, I do," I fibbed, watching their eyes light up.

When they visited in early summer one of our magical games was to chase fireflies in my backyard. Well past their bedtime, they were seven and four, their reprieve was to frolic with the 'fairies.'

"I think they really are fairies, Nana," Stella proclaimed, "Don't you?"

How could I deny them such innocent imagination?

"Yes," I stated, with that twinkle in my eye.

It spurred my own curiosity, this phenomenon, and I started reading about the winged insects. The mellifluous glowworms, the Eastern US blue ghost, displays a quality called bioluminescence. It's the humidity, the Midwest, marshy, wooded habitat that engenders their propagation. They live a mere three weeks to two months, all of an inch in size with that bright firelight luring attention, attracting a mate. I want that, the ability to transform into a magical being. A two month relationship would not be hard to sustain. Could I have light, enough pride in my own luminescence to take flight, emitting a glowing magnet of fascination to my sphere?

My grateful heart swells watching my scampering grandchildren collect a dozen of the treasures into a Mason jar, careful not to injure the delicate gems.

"Do you really think they are fairies?" they ask, again wanting the affirmation of faith.

"If you believe it, that's all you need," I assure.

They'll learn realities soon enough, facts that steal their light, tamp the fire, challenge hope, awakening to bitter truths. Right now, the pollen of life, the sweet nectar feeds these youngsters with pure simplicity, filling their dreams this balmy summer night.

"Nana, Nana, look," they whisper, holding the jar up to my face.

My outward appearance may not glow but my inner light, breathing in their joy fans flames of love. I make a conscious decision to shine my light, to let the fire of life warm, comfort, burn off the chaff and incinerate negative toxins. In their few years of childhood I promise to believe in elves, love, luck, solstice, stars and mysterious enchantment.

I once heard someone say, "Those who don't believe in magic will never find it." I believe.

—Lynne Zotalis

Wood-fired Loaves

My off-the-grid experience,
my early twenties, taught invaluable lessons,
mostly the hard way. Boiling water to purify it,
digging a two foot hole in the ground for cold storage,
and cooking with wood
consumed the humble life for seven years.
My approach
to mastering the volatile culinary proficiency,
understanding its quirks and nuances,
employed much trial and error.
I discovered the differences in wood;
pine, oak, hickory, a crucial key,
producing a marked variation in the outcome.
Whether swift and blistering or temperate and sustained,
I learned to adeptly calculate the size
and proportions of various species.

Initially, fire was not my friend, burning me
alongside my sad offerings until necessity
proved an able teacher, if not judge.
My piece de resistance was loaf after loaf
of scrumptious whole wheat bread,
risen to perfection, before sliding into the oven
with an evenly monitored fire,
my keen eye verifying the 350 degree temperature
not allowing it to dip or exceed more than a few degrees
at the expense or even demise of the precious loaves.

At the appointed time I rotated them
from a bottom shelf to top,
switching loaves from left to right
insuring a gorgeous golden brown,
wafting aroma throughout the log cabin.
Four loaves a week—the first all but devoured
as soon as it was cool enough to handle.

Slathered with butter as slices handily disappeared,
tell-tale rivulets dripping down chins.
Labor intensive, exceptionally rewarding,
those simpler times still elicit wishes
for my cast iron cook stove.

Alas, reason prevails.

—Lynne Zotalis

Then I Met the Burned Children

I have lived by the same story
for a long time now—a tale of conquest.
Then I met the burned children.

They appeared on a trail of rock and mud.
Snapped trees blocked my passage.
With the forest gone, I could see out into the valley
to the desert's plains and mountains.
The children never kept still—perhaps they were made of smoke.

The land had endured logging
and our stubborn defeat of small fires
that would speed through undergrowth.
The hillsides held nothing now but black, barren stems.
A clogged stream carried ashes and grit and dead wood.

The children were dark clouds.
With the forest gone,
 rain meant breakneck floods–
in the valley below, anguished people labored
to steer the flash-water past their houses.

I longed to love the burned children,
the people, the dead trees, their buried seeds.
On that ruined trail, I dreamed myself into a different life,
one of sharing. Of nurture.
As a token, I took a charred branch.

I have lived by the same story
for a long time now—a tale of conquest—
but I met the burned children.

—Leonore Hildebrandt

Instauration to Illumination

Rising from the cinders
of these roaring 2020's,
the smoldering spirit within
emerges with wings.
Not made of feathers and fluff,
but of glowing flames,
just enough to set the world afire.

No cause for destruction
or smoky devastation,
just sparks and tinder
of healing instauration.

With kindling of compassion
and civility, sparking
embers of empathy—
fan the flames of transformation.

World illuminated.

—Shelly Barnett

Hair on Fire

An empty vessel
I am cradled in intentions

weighted down by lists
and obligations

mired in that delicate dance
between forward motion
and regenerative stillness

a nagging sense of
losing ground

but carried by
earnest optimism
coloring all possibilities

until
with tresses aflame
the fire within
demands a poem

—Pamela Warren Williams

Fire in the Bones

Words smolder inside me
and I feed on outside tinder,
lighting a wildfire of longing.

Lover,
How many houses
must we burn,
to clear the path
to our Altar of We?

Flames in each other's eyes
draw us even deeper,
illumining our desires
from the fire in our bones.

Candles flicker continuously,
each one an offering
to enkindle our faith
in each other.

Emblazoned at the altar
we sacrifice nothing,
yet give ourselves completely
to the fire in our bones.

—Shelly Barnett

Air

Birdsong

Imagine

that one melody

was all we could or would

or knew how to do? The same

    lilting song every waking hour,

at dawn   and all day long,

    tiny lungs filling again and again

  to sing soul's sweet refrain.

I take heed   settling into evening,

  first star slips from dusk's canopy,

  illuminates quieting notes

that cannot be silenced

    just yet. A deep

    cleansing breath sustains one more chorus.

—Lynne Zotalis

Breathing

reminded to exhale

create space for renewal

necessary to refill the well

replenishing the bounty

of joy

of love

of kindness

animating this being

essence of vitality

to dispense as with laughter

——Pamela Warren Williams

Breathless Universe/Seven Planetary Haiku

Becoming the Sun
when I choose to fearlessly
live the rest of days.

      We awake with her
      Sister Morningstar Venus.
      Blessing of brightness.

            Dust devils swirling
            Cold desert, two-mooned planet.
            Rocky, rust-red Mars.

You might laugh at this—
Did you know on Uranus
it's raining diamonds?

      Great red spot shrinking,
      yet devouring other storms,
      Jupiter rising.

            Karmic ball of gas
            I'm two years old on Saturn
            adorned with ringlets.

We dance with the moon
Uplifting our arms, twirling,
defying darkness.

—Shelly Barnett

Suspended

The first snow surprises, expanding
   ideas of distance, casting the trees in profile
     omitting much of the field

but on foot
   I still feel the same abundance
     of root, sand, and rock

the way I watch you at rest
   and find another face beneath
     softly familiar and yet unseen

and now the snow dancers
   flex the air
     mingling laces and jade into dark

stretching like winter—long into longing—
   and lazily floating a fleece
     for the newborn night.

—Leonore Hildebrandt

Earth Sans Air

Some believe that air
keeps the sky from falling down to earth.

Would stars lay at our feet,
trod upon and stuck to soles
of those too busy to notice?

Would souls of our loved ones
wandering across Earth's limbo,
be searching for their place in the blackness?

Air, precious air
you are inspiration of
strength supporting wings of flight—
of birds and machines.
You stiffen sails of ships
and carry kites on your gentle currents.
You move resistant waters of stagnation,
coerce trees to wave their branches,
and animate clay of every living being.

And Air—
you are the home of souls
after the dissolution of bodies.

Your sacredness treasured by all
as you whisper your fears
all the way to the universe.

—Shelly Barnett

It's in the Air

It's in the air, finer than dust.
Denser than smoke.

We move our beach chairs to higher ground
for a deeper breath—adaptation. Mitigation.

It dissipates into borderlands—
a stranger's lungs. The thinning heft of forest.

Leisurely we discuss the animated climate graphs,
bright circles that crazily flit and expand.

It's in the air. It spills from the highest mountains,
invades the finest capillaries.

We might have known it—life—
a butterfly's journey, a sunlit patch of land.

It's the air—the wind's
eventful, awesome equilibrium.

—Leonore Hildebrandt

Loquacious Limbs

one must take notice

stark and austere, slicing through vapid sky

expression extending

along   bent lines

crooked measures

the musical staff

of nature scale of echoes

reaching   thrusting

upward

outward   finally

released

plunging down

liberated

swaying slightly

no drag

from leaves long gone

no whispers

singing   night along

      to dawn

only an occasional creak

      and crack

    from   indolent branches   able no longer   to hold fast   time

to die   to dash against iced earth   crumbling inevitably to dust

washed down to aquifer   sucked into roots

      to dance summer's soft harmony   swishing

amongst vibrant emerald canopy   expiring fresh oxygen

      sluicing our very life blood

        sighing back into awaiting lungs.

—Lynne Zotalis

African Drums

The djembe resounds. It throbs and yells.
It cries, come here, come now.

The players, seated in a circle,
rouse the air to welcome strangers.

A queen? I fall into my mother tongue
—mumbled words, inaudible—

drum of mourning, drum of dwelling.
Slap and tone. Flesh and bone?

As a child, I would long to be older.
Now my temples seem to burst—

no dying spell, no death-knell—but an outcry
crying out, for what—for what—

an upwelling—joy, joy—and then a dancer's
eloquence, a whirl, a laughing shout.

—Leonore Hildebrandt

Racing with Joy

I race the howling wind across town—
not too far, I note happily. A game, in a way,
as I really would not mind getting wet,
just dancing up the hill from the car.
That clever orange wind-proof umbrella
still a novice accessory. I admire the array of virga
in the distance and study the many layers and hues of gray
adorning the fall sky, my joy ongoing over living
at this height, where the elevation displays
the oncoming weather so clearly.

Exhilarated by the afternoon's accomplishments,
I hear some Italian aria in my head as a soundtrack to
this brief sprint home. Have I perhaps watched too many
filmed car chases? I still know to appear sedate as I
wheel through campus, comforted by the officer
at his customary post in the fifteen-mph zone.

They say that new skills are the key to the vital mind
rather than more scrabble, wordle, or mah-jongg,
but a different hurdle as often as possible.
Is Photoshop within my grasp?
Even the silly upgrade with too many
bells and whistles for its own good?
I accept the challenge.

—Pamela Warren Williams

Water

The Bath

Visions of some classical painting featuring an odalisque
lounging sensually on sumptuous embroidered textiles,
feeling baptized, cared for, and quite sated.
But that part was afterwards.

Scented with various exotic essential oils,
you offer sacraments of healing, nurturing, balancing.

Baking soda for baby-soft skin.
Salts to disengage the tired muscles and tired mind,
and to float all the worries on downstream.

The array of warm, cream-colored pillars
and twinkling votives atop the protective wall
just outside the open French doors,
blessing me with their glow.

And bubbles, of course, simply to delight me.
There would have been beverage service.
A mug of that wild berry tea.
Or a humoring glass of cooling chardonnay.

Sorrow that I am unable to remember
the accompanying soundtrack—
something chosen with great care, I am certain.
Perhaps a Taizé or something mysteriously melodic.

Bathed in reverie, the mind chooses what to hold...
Or sometimes to tenderly offer up again years later.
Was that intentional, I muse?

I understand that joy can be triggered
just as sadness. Surely a worthy practice.

—Pamela Warren Williams

Missing the Pacific

Standing where earth meets water,
and water meets changing colors of sky,
I can almost see the turn of the world.
Seeking solace, I allow rhythms of the ocean
to become soothing vibrations in my being.

Just as quickly as waves roar to the shore,
they are whisked away in whispers,
leaving trashy treasures and salty tears
glistening at my sandy toe-tips.

Seaweed cloaked driftwood,
agates and broken shells,
rusty bits, beach glass and pottery shards—
messengers of earth.
One by one,
my pockets fill with imagined stories
and surplus grains of sand.
Seaweed stays behind,
longing for surf to carry it out to sea,
in search of another soaked surface to embrace.

I wander water's edge
from sunrise to darkness,
speaking only to the Pacific Ocean—
healer without words.

—Shelly Barnett

Octopus Teacher

Entwined vulnerability in the ethereal kelp forest,
with its evocative light and secrets.
Defying color and texture possibilities
and sensory miracles times two thousand.
The knowing of our connectivity.

Watching without interference the predation
of a pyjama shark true to its very nature.
Respect for the offering of a life
to complete the circle,
birthing half a million tiny hopes.
The diligence required to truly know
the complexities, the hierarchy
of this otherworldly realm.

Trust, as a mantra,
patiently and relentlessly driving
the flow of time evolving forward.
To merely pass through this diorama,
a rare permission.

To connect these worlds, extraordinary.
Physically touched, as well as psychically.
Dedication to this deep gnosis,
voyeur to the construction of another's armor
while shedding all of one's own.
The rewarding gentleness
a worthy goal to be tutored.

—Pamela Warren Williams

A Sunken Garden

In my dream you were standing
  at the edge of a land so wide
    we could see the distant hours fuse.

You were the river's invisible currents
  and its surface—a sky-mirror.
    The water turned dark—

submerged, we floated among slow-spinning
  water lilies, their weightless linkage.
    Later, facing one another, we felt no need

to choose our beginnings and endings.
  There was no ceremony, no witness,
    but in the river's depth, our fingers touched—

fingers only, ever so lightly. In my dream
  you were the pale rocks lining the water.

—Leonore Hildebrandt

Fragments

one   single tear   falling
a droplet   exudes from rocky crag
to relieve the pressure
trying to safeguard
fragments of a heart

never again
will I
nor could I
endure such annihilation

vigilantly I guard and defend
owning the bruised
and pummeled
fragments of a heart

cannot allow another access
water splashing my palm   water that cannot be held
escapes through my fingers   pressed tightly to hold it back

twisted remnants remain
like shattered
fragments of a heart

try   try to gather
elusive mist   from scorched clay
the protective shield   once breached
still defensive   tightly bound armored
fragments of a heart

—Lynne Zotalis

Gathering Tears

Bodies of water
lying in wait,
dying of waste.
Crying, crying.

Hands dip below
undulating fluid surfaces,
filling finger formed vessels
with liquid of life.

Hold earth's gift briefly
dripping from palm cups
to ground.

What remains on skin
is clearly blood
and tears of Mother,
holy water
of deepest messages.

—Shelly Barnett

Reassembly

So, can one actually
transmute/translate/transform
fear into awe?

Water into wine, right?

Can I?

The collaborative intentions
fire frantically
as we each regroup,
reassembling ourselves
in new arrangements,
reaching out for
the connection
that we have
missed
in our assorted
isolations.

Can we arrive at
a new form of relating?

Will you collaborate?

New realities,
new truths.

New ways
to lift each other up.

—Pamela Warren Willliams

To Think Like Water

The landscaper walks the sloping terrain,
hoping to think like water.
Fitful run-offs converge, carving the ground
down to bedrock, gutting the road in summer.
He says, these times call for handheld tools.

Water is bold—
it scrapes notations deep into the planet's crust.
Raindrops—a menace? Too many of them. Too few.
We've tried to break rivers, harness their force.
We've held ribbon cuttings, celebrating concrete.

Water outlives us—
it rises from the earth, it billows and swirls
then returns to the mountains that crown this desert.
He says, earth-movers can't block the water's fearsome
gravity. Bulldozers won't outwit it.

Water pools—
the landscaper brings a shovel and a rake.
He lays out a berm for a shallow basin with a wide outlet.
He thinks of rain, the quiver of rivulets,
seed beds, a calmness saturating down to the roots.

—Leonore Hildebrandt

Circle of Belonging

ripples of water   moisture laden circles

diversity exemplified   all marvelously extending

from and through one another

young   aged   diminutive   ample, feel the energy

generated fluently   perpetuating   placid fluctuation

balanced dance, swirling life continuum, in and of itself,

able, as an aggregate, to transcend divisiveness

with inclusive overtures

radiating images from black to white

obscure to pure   from center,

the middle effecting each sphere

all unique,   unity revealing

simplicity of purpose

for those of us who choose to see it

the invisible bond

holding each other

in that place of belonging.

—Lynne Zotalis

It's the way we lift one another up that defines us in our community, and that defines us as a community.

—Stewart S. Warren

Biographies

Shelly Barnett

Shelly "Badassia" Barnett moved to Southwest New Mexico, longing for warmth and sunshine after half of her life in the Pacific Northwest. As long as there are trees—Poet-trees, Creativi-trees, and others with fruit, like peaches, life is good. Writing since she was seven years old, some of her pieces were featured in school publications and then, local arts magazines in the NW. After twenty plus years of a writing hiatus, she revisited and reinvented her poetic style when she moved to Albuquerque. Falling in love with Open Mic and Spoken Word, she dances the line of both when she performs. A mother, an activist, a teacher of our youth, an artist and a poetry possibilitarian, she speaks her truth, even if her voice shakes.

Leonore Hildebrandt

Leonore Hildebrandt is the author of the poetry collections *The Work at Hand*, *The Next Unknown*, and *Where You Happen to Be*. Her poems and translations have appeared in the Cafe Review, Cerise Press, the Cimarron Review, Denver Quarterly, The Fiddlehead, Harpur Palate, Poetry Daily, Rhino, and the Sugar House Review, among other journals. She was nominated several times for a Pushcart Prize. Some of her poetry and original songs can be found at http://leonorehildebrandt.com. Originally from Germany, Leonore lives off-the-grid in Harrington, Maine, and spends the winter in Silver City, New Mexico.

Pamela Warren Williams

Pamela Warren Williams is a poet, publisher, and visual artist, searching for the poignant truths, with provocation from heart-breaking beauty to the current pain in our culture and following the ties that either bind us or tear us apart. Her poems rich in irony, compassion, and challenge, she invites us along on the Fool's Journey, embracing the gifts of vulnerability. Her publishing company, Mercury HeartLink, www.heartlink.com promotes positive social impact. Her poems have appeared in Live Out Loud, Poetry Lovers ePub, *Lummox 6-9* anthologies, *Walls* and *Survival*, Poets Speak anthologies, Writinginawomansvoice.blogspot.com, and *Fixed and Free* anthologies. Her books, *Hair on Fire*, and *You, Always Near, the Stewart Poems* are available on amazon: http://amzn.to/2eD5lxL

Lynne Zotalis

Lynne Zotalis is an award-winning author, poet and chairperson for the Silver City chapter of the NM State Poetry Society. She has published short stories and poetry in Tuck Magazine, an online human rights journal, Writinginawoman'svoice.blogspot.com, The Poetic Bond VII, VIII, IX, X, Lyrical Iowa, and NMSPS anthology *Glissando*. She has contributed to numerous anthologies including *Turning Points: Discovering Meaning and Passion in Turbulent Times*. Ms. Zotalis' poetry collection, *Mysterious Existence*, as well as *Saying Goodbye to Chuck*, a daily journal to enunciate the readers' personal grief process are available on Amazon. Her memoir/creative nonfiction, *Hippie at Heart, What I Used to Be, I Still Am* won a Firebird Book Award and was a finalist in the Best Book Awards https://www.amazon.com/dp/B08DC6GZ7T